Parks and Gardens

Charlotte Guillain

Raintree

www.raintreepublishers.co.uk
Visit our website to find out more information about Raintree books.

To order:

☎ Phone 0845 6044371

📄 Fax +44 (0) 1865 312263

🖵 Email myorders@capstonepub.co.uk

Customers from outside the UK please telephone +44 1865 312262

Raintree is an imprint of Capstone Global Library Limited, a company incorporated in England and Wales having its registered office at 7 Pilgrim Street, London, EC4V 6LB – Registered company number: 6695582

"Raintree" is a registered trademark of Pearson Education Limited, under licence to Capstone Global Library Limited

Text © Capstone Global Library Limited 2010
First published in hardback in 2010
The moral rights of the proprietor have been asserted.

Edited by Charlotte Guillain, Nancy Dickmann, and Catherine Veitch
Designed by Joanna Hinton-Malivoire
Picture research by Elizabeth Alexander and Ruth Blair
Production by Victoria Fitzgerald
Originated by Capstone Global Library Ltd
Printed and bound in China by Leo Paper Products

ISBN 978 0 431 17243 9
14 13 12 11 10
10 9 8 7 6 5 4 3 2 1

British Library Cataloguing in Publication Data
Guillain, Charlotte.
Parks and gardens. -- (Nature trails)
577.5'54-dc22

Acknowledgements
We would like to thank the following for permission to reproduce photographs: Corbis pp. **7** (© Toby Melville/Reuters), **9** (© Gideon Mendel), **25** (© Roger Tidman); iStockphoto pp. **6** (© V. J. Matthew), **8**, **12** (© Roger Whiteway), **13 top right** (© Andrzej Tokarski), **16** (© Joseph Calev), **18** (© Simone van den Berg), **20** (© Andrew Howe), **21 bottom left** (© Donall O Cleirigh), **22** (© Karel Broz), **24** (© Martin Trebbin), **29 top left** (© Andrew Howe), **29 top right** (© Andrew Howe), **14 top left** (© Roger Whiteway), **14 right**, **14 bottom left** (© Oliver Malms); Photolibrary pp. **4-5** (Panorama Stock), **10** (Garden Picture Library), **15** (Imagebroker.net), **17** (age footstock), **19** (Animals Animals), **26** (Garden Picture Library), **27** (Photononstop); Shutterstock pp. **13 top left** (Robyn Mackenzie), **13 middle** (Valenta), **13 bottom left** (Lfoto), **21 top left** (Sebastian Knight), **21 right** (Stratila), **23** (Mircea Bezergheanu), **29 bottom left** (Sebastian Knight), **29 bottom right** (Anatoli Dubkov).

Cover photograph of Parterre Garden and Hedge Maze at Hatfield House reproduced with permission of Corbis (© Harpur Garden Library).

The publisher would like to thank Emma Shambrook for her assistance in the preparation of this book.

Every effort has been made to contact copyright holders of material reproduced in this book. Any omissions will be rectified in subsequent printings if notice is given to the publisher.

Contents

What are parks and gardens? 4

Different parks and gardens. 6

Changes through the year 8

Exploring parks and gardens 10

Trees in parks and gardens 12

Park and garden flowers. 14

Park and garden insects 16

Park and garden minibeasts. 18

Birds in parks and gardens 20

More park and garden birds 22

Park and garden mammals 24

Parks and gardens in danger 26

More things to do. 28

Glossary. 30

Find out more 31

Index 32

Any words appearing in the text in bold, **like this**, are explained in the glossary.

What are parks and gardens?

There are many different parks and gardens in Britain. Many homes have their own gardens, yards, or window boxes. Parks and public gardens are bigger open spaces for many people to share.

In this book, the Signpost boxes ask you to find out more about animals and plants. Ask an adult to help you find information in books at school, in the library, or on the Internet.

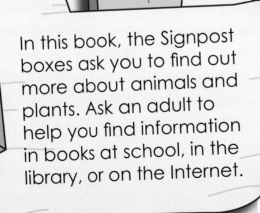

Parks and gardens are types of **habitat**. A habitat is a place where animals and plants live. Many different animals and plants live in British parks and gardens.

Different parks and gardens

There are many types, shapes, and sizes of garden and park. Many homes have gardens where people grow flowers or vegetables or play and relax on lawns and **patios**. **Botanical gardens** are places where people can see many unusual plants growing together.

Some parks are in the grounds of **stately homes** and can be more **formal**.

There are many different parks in Britain. Most towns and cities have parks that are large open spaces where people can walk, relax, and play. These parks often have many plants and trees for people to enjoy.

Changes through the year

If you visit parks and gardens at different times of the year, you will see many changes. In spring there are flowers such as snowdrops, daffodils, and crocuses on the ground. In summer many colourful flowers grow and the leafy trees give shade from the sun.

In spring you can see **blossom** on the trees.

In autumn the trees look beautiful as the leaves change colour from green to orange, yellow, and red. In winter there are only bright berries on the bare branches. **Evergreen** trees stay green all year round in many parks and gardens.

Exploring parks and gardens

It is easy for everyone to visit and explore a park or garden. You might be lucky enough to have your own garden. Otherwise you can visit your local park and hunt for plants and animals in all seasons.

There are lots of places for creatures to hide in a garden. If you move stones to look underneath, always put them back in the same place.

What to take with you

- ✓ A notebook
- ✓ A pencil
- ✓ A magnifying glass
- ✓ A digital camera

STAY SAFE !

- If you are visiting a park, always go with an adult and check you are allowed to explore all parts of the park.
- Never disturb animals or pull up plants.

Trees in parks and gardens

Many types of trees and **shrubs** grow in parks and gardens. Children look for conkers under horse chestnut trees in autumn. Sycamore trees drop their seeds in pairs so they twirl like helicopters.

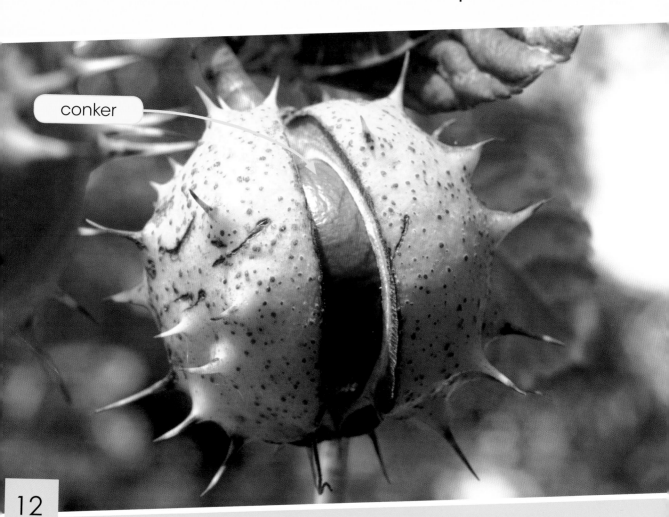

conker

Older parkland can have **ancient** trees, such as oaks. Many gardens have fruit trees such as cherry, plum, and apple, which produce fruit in the summer and autumn.

Some common leaves

silver birch

oak

horse chestnut

sycamore

Can you find out about three more trees?
- beech
- privet
- fir

Park and garden flowers

buttercup

daisy

lavender

In parks and gardens there are wild flowers and flowers that gardeners have planted. Common wild flowers are buttercups, clover, and daisies. Butterflies and bees visit wild flowers and help to **pollinate** them.

Gardeners plant flowers that also **attract** insects, such as buddleia bushes, red valerian, lavender, and primula. Flowers are brightly coloured and smell nice to attract insects.

buddleia bush

Park and garden insects

Many different types of insects live and feed among the plants in a park or garden. Butterflies feed on the flowers they find there. Some butterflies lay their eggs on nettles and their caterpillars eat the nettle leaves.

Look for ladybirds on roses. They feed on the bugs that eat the plants, so gardeners like them.

Cuckoo spit keeps the young insects safe as they grow.

On some plants in spring and early summer you might find cuckoo spit. This is a white, frothy material that looks a bit like spit. It is made by an insect called a froghopper that lays its eggs on plants.

Park and garden minibeasts

Parks and gardens are full of other **minibeasts**. Try looking under stones for woodlice and earthworms. Earthworms will quickly burrow back into the soil unless a hungry bird spots them.

woodlouse

On a wet morning you can often spot slugs and snails hunting for juicy leaves. Look for caterpillars on plants in early summer. You might find other insects on the bark of trees.

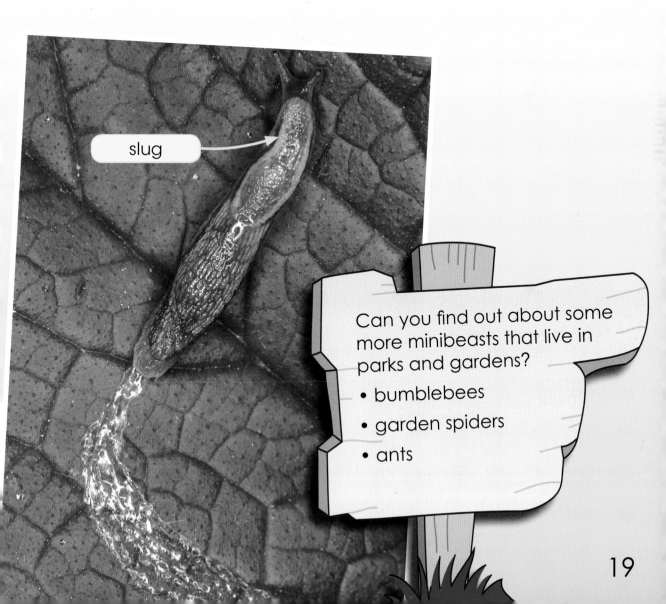

slug

Can you find out about some more minibeasts that live in parks and gardens?

- bumblebees
- garden spiders
- ants

19

Birds in parks and gardens

Many birds come to gardens and parks looking for insects and plants to eat. Common British garden birds you can see all year round include blackbirds, blue tits, house sparrows, starlings, and chaffinches.

If you have a garden you can put out food and water and watch the birds that visit.

Also look out for robins, wood pigeons, and green finches. Listen to their different songs and you might start to recognize them.

This is a food chain. It shows what different creatures eat.

blackbird

slug

lettuce

More park and garden birds

Parks and gardens are good **habitats** for birds to build their nests. Birds use twigs, **moss**, and leaves to make nests where they lay eggs in spring. The tall trees, bushes, and buildings in parks and gardens are safe places for nests.

Summer visitors such as these swallows use mud to build their nests under the roofs of buildings.

If you are lucky you might see more rare birds, such as woodpeckers, song thrushes, siskins, and goldcrests.

woodpecker

Can you find out about some more garden birds?

- waxwings
- yellowhammers
- redpolls
- goldfinches

23

Park and garden mammals

Small mammals, such as foxes, hedgehogs, squirrels, and rabbits often visit parks and gardens. They come to eat the plants and **minibeasts** that live and grow there. Squirrels climb trees looking for seeds and nuts. Hedgehogs come out at night to eat worms, slugs, and beetles.

The soil in a park or garden is good for digging. Moles hunt for worms and leave molehills behind.

Foxes often visit gardens in towns and cities at night. In the wild, foxes eat birds and minibeasts, but they come to gardens to find food in people's dustbins. Other **nocturnal** visitors include mice and rats.

Parks and gardens in danger

Many animals, birds, and **minibeasts** visit parks and gardens. They need these **habitats** to live. When gardens are covered in concrete for cars to park, there are fewer plants to feed on.

Sometimes gardeners use **chemicals** that can kill animals such as hedgehogs.

You can help look after parks and gardens by taking care when you visit them. Always leave things as you find them. If you have a garden you could plant flowers that butterflies and bees like to visit and put out food and water for birds in the winter.

Never leave litter behind because this can hurt animals.

More things to do

There are a lot more things you can do in parks and gardens.

Count and record

Can you count the different types of coloured flower in part of your park or garden? Record them in a **bar chart** like this one. Do you notice whether bees and butterflies prefer some colours?

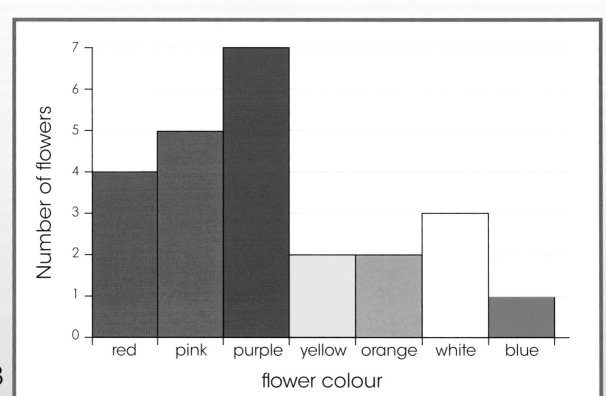

Do a bird survey

Spend an hour in your local park or watching your garden and do a survey of the birds that visit.

1 Use a bird identification book or print a guide off the Internet to help you recognize the birds.

2 Count the highest number of any type of bird you see at any one time and make a note of all the types of birds you see during the hour.

3 If you date your survey you could repeat it next year and see if things have changed.

blackbird

sparrow

bluetit

starling

Glossary

ancient very old

attract make something come close

bar chart diagram where numbers of things are shown by different coloured blocks

blossom flower, usually on a fruit tree

botanical garden garden that has been specially planted with different types of plant

chemical special substance. Gardeners use chemicals to kill pests.

evergreen tree or plant that has leaves all year round

formal carefully arranged and special

habitat natural home of a group of plants and animals

minibeasts small animals, such as spiders, snails, and worms

moss small, green, spongy plants that grow in damp places

nocturnal active during the night

patio paved area by a house

pollinate take pollen from one flower to another, so new flowers can grow

shrub small, woody plant

stately home large house or mansion

Find out more

Books to read

Garden Encyclopedia, Rufus Bellamy (A & C Black, 2009)

Look What I Found!: In the Garden, G. Barker and
P. Humphreys (Franklin Watts, 2005)

Websites and organizations

RSPB
www.rspb.org.uk
On the RSPB website you can identify the birds you see
and find out more about looking after the wildlife in our
parks and gardens.

Wildlife Trust
www.wildlifetrusts.org
Your local Wildlife Trust will know about the parks in your
area that you can visit.

www.greenflagaward.org.uk
Your local council manages the parks in your area and
may have someone who can help you explore. Visit this
website to find the best parks in your area.

Index

bar charts 28
birds 20–23, 25, 27, 29
blossom 8
botanical gardens 6
butterflies and bees 14, 15, 16, 27, 28

caterpillars 16, 19
chemicals 26
conkers 12
cuckoo spit 17

evergreen trees 9
exploring parks and gardens 10–11

flowers 8, 14–15, 16, 28
food chain 21
foxes 25
fruit trees 13

habitats 5, 22, 26
hedgehogs 24, 26

insects 14, 15, 16–17

ladybirds 16
leaves 13

litter 27

mammals 24–25
minibeasts 18–19, 24, 25
moles 24

nocturnal animals 25

pollination 14
protecting parks and gardens 10, 11, 27

safety 11
seasons 8–9
slugs and snails 19, 21, 24
squirrels 24
stately homes 7
surveys 29
swallows 22

trees and shrubs 8, 9, 12–13

wild flowers 14
woodlice 18
woodpeckers 23
worms 18, 24